DOING WHAT
I DO BEST

Russell Myers

FAWCETT GOLD MEDAL • NEW YORK

Library of Congress Catalog Card Number: 84-90887

ISBN 0-449-12491-6

Manufactured in the United States of America

First Ballantine Books Edition: August 1984

10 9 8 7 6 5 4 3 2 1

TERMITES!

GAYLORD, DO YOU BELIEVE
THAT HUMANS EVOLVED
FROM LOWER CREATURES?

A school
of fish

A herd
of cattle

MOO

MOO
TO YOU

MOO
TO
YOU
TOO

A pride
of lions

An excess
of witches

RUSSELL
MYERS

RUSSELL
MYERS

YOU ARE FAT, STUPID, LAZY, SELFISH, DIRTY, UGLY...

OH GO ON WITH YOU!

CLOP

ALL THAT ATTENTION MAKES A GIRL SO GIDDY!

RUSSELL MYERS

RUSSELL MYERS

RUSSELL MYERS

RUSSELL MYERS

RUSSELL MYERS

RUSSELL MYERS

Wolves are smart,
Wolves are sweet.

Wolves are orderly
And quite neat.

We're also kind
And very thrifty...

Dogs ain't bad
But wolves are **nifty!**

RUSSELL MYERS

I SAVED A SNOWBALL FROM LAST WINTER!

WHAT SHOULD I DO WITH IT?

RUSSELL MYERS

THIS TURNED OUT BETTER THAN I EXPECTED!

HI, MOM! IT'S GAYLORD! GOTTA RUN! BYE!

I CAN NEVER MAKE A LONG-DISTANCE CALL WITHOUT WORRYING ABOUT COST!

RUSSELL MYERS

RUSSELL MYERS

RUSSELL MYERS

THE SOUND OF
MOOOOOOSIC

RUSSELL MYERS

RUSSELL MYERS

Dear Mother Nature;
I'm bored today.

Please do something
interesting.

CRACK

Thank you,
Irwin

SLAM

RUSSELL
MYERS

RUSSELL MYERS

RUSSELL MYERS

BUG SPRAY!

BUZZZZZZZZzzz

OH OH...

RUSSELL MYERS

AWW... POUTIN' ABOUT BEIN' BALD, GAYLORD?

LOTS OF FAMOUS PEOPLE HAVE BEEN BALD!

MUSSOLINI... JACK THE RIPPER...

I ALWAYS START OUT **TRYIN'** TO BE NICE BUT IT JUST AIN'T NO **FUN!**

RUSSELL MYERS

IRWIN GETS TALKED INTO THINGS TOO EASILY!

WHAT NOW?

HE'S JOINED A *CULT*!

RUSSELL MYERS

I WONDER IF SOMEWHERE
THERE'S A TREATMENT
PROGRAM FOR MALTED
MILK BALL
ABUSERS?

RATTLE
RATTLE

RUSSELL MYERS

-RUSSELL MYERS

RUSSELL MYERS

RUSSELL MYERS

YOU CAN PREDICT THE WEATHER BY AN ANIMAL'S COAT!

THE HEAVIER HIS COAT, THE COLDER THE COMING WINTER WILL BE!

OH OH...

RUSSELL MYERS

SACK OF QUARTERS

PADDED STOOL...

COFFEE...

THUMB GUARDS

I'M ALL SET FOR MY FAVORITE SPORT!

SPORT?

VIDEO GAMES

RUSSELL MYERS

RUSSELL MYERS

WE'VE GOT TO WORK OUT OUR SIGNALS BETTER!

IRWIN, I'VE SAVED US A FORTUNE IN GARBAGE COLLECTION FEES!

I BOUGHT A **GOAT** TO EAT ALL THE TRASH!

DOWN BOY!

RUSSELL MYERS

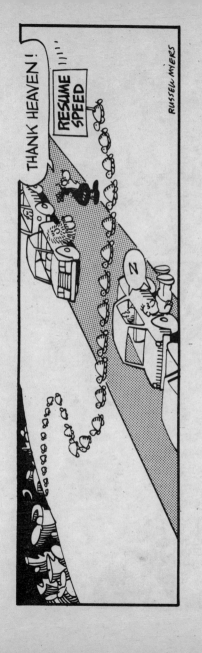

The second I married Rip Van Winkle he fell asleep!

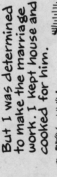

But I was determined to make the marriage work. I kept house and cooked for him.

HOW'S THE SOUP, DEAR?

ZZZNRF

RUSSELL MYERS